HAL LEONARD

PIANO METHOD

PIANO FOR KIDS SONGBOOK

12 Popular Piano Solos for Beginners

ARRANGED BY JENNIFER LINN

To access audio visit:
www.halleonard.com/mylibrary

"Enter Code"
8093-8078-7452-2238

ISBN 978-1-4950-8850-6

Visit Hal Leonard Online at
www.halleonard.com

Contact us:
Hal Leonard
7777 West Bluemound Road
Milwaukee, WI 53213
Email: info@halleonard.com

In Europe, contact:
Hal Leonard Europe Limited
42 Wigmore Street
Marylebone, London, W1U 2RN
Email: info@halleonardeurope.com

In Australia, contact:
Hal Leonard Australia Pty. Ltd.
4 Lentara Court
Cheltenham, Victoria, 3192 Australia
Email: info@halleonard.com.au

INTRODUCTION

Beginners will love being able to play popular songs right away! *Piano for Kids Songbook* is a supplementary companion to the *Piano for Kids Method Book* as the songs begin with pre-staff notation (note names inside the note heads) and progress in like manner to reading notes on the staff. The pop arrangements reinforce concepts learned in the method book. From classic songs like "Do-Re-Mi" and "Linus and Lucy" to contemporary hits like "All of Me" or "Can't Stop the Feeling," kids will enjoy playing songs that everyone knows (even Mom and Dad!).

 # ABOUT THE AUDIO

To access the accompanying audio, simply go to **www.halleonard.com/ mylibrary** and enter the code found on page 1 of this book. This will grant you instant access to every file. You can download to your computer, tablet, or phone, or stream the audio live—and you can also use our *PLAYBACK+* multi-functional audio player to slow down or speed up the tempo, change keys, or set loop points. This feature is available exclusively from Hal Leonard and is included with the price of this book!

For technical support, please email support@halleonard.com

CONTENTS

Pre-Staff

On Staff

HOW TO SIT AT THE PIANO

- Sit tall on the front half of the bench.
- Lean slightly forward.
- Keep your feet flat on the floor.
- Your knees should be only slightly under the keys.
- Your elbows should be higher than the keyboard level.
- Keep your shoulders relaxed.

GOOD HAND POSITION

- Make sure your wrist and back of the hand form a straight line.
- Curve your fingers so that only your fingertips are touching the keys.
- Use the side tip of your thumb.
- Keep your wrist relaxed and flexible.

FINGER NUMBERS

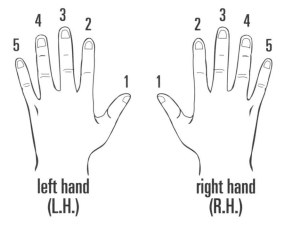

left hand
(L.H.)

right hand
(R.H.)

- Each finger is assigned a number.
- Place your palms together with your fingertips touching.

  Tap 1's (thumbs)

  Tap 2's

  Tap 3's

  Tap 4's

  Tap 5's

- FINGERING: The finger numbers will appear above and below the music notes. These numbers are known as the fingering and are to be followed exactly.

THE KEYBOARD

The keyboard consists of white and black keys. The black keys are arranged in groups of twos and threes.

- Circle all the 2 black-key groups and box all the 3 black-key groups below.

- Play all the 2 black-key groups on your keyboard with your L.H., using fingers 2 and 3.

- Play all the 3 black-key groups with your R.H., using fingers 2, 3, 4.

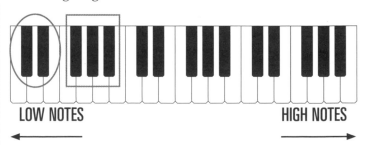

LOW NOTES   HIGH NOTES

KEYBOARD REVIEW

Write in the key names for all the white keys below.

REVIEW MATCH

Draw a line to connect each musical symbol to its correct name.

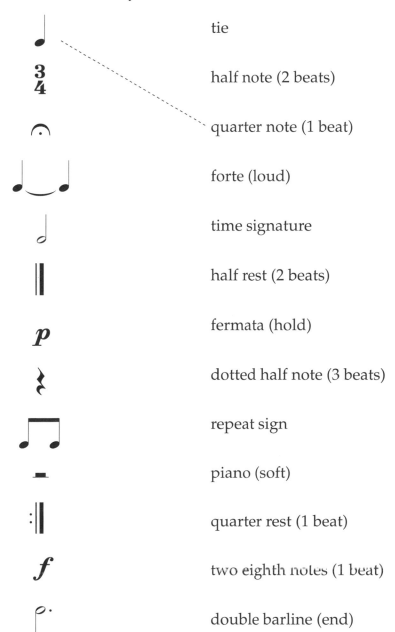

tie

half note (2 beats)

quarter note (1 beat)

forte (loud)

time signature

half rest (2 beats)

fermata (hold)

dotted half note (3 beats)

repeat sign

piano (soft)

quarter rest (1 beat)

two eighth notes (1 beat)

double barline (end)

IT'S A SMALL WORLD

from Disney Parks' "it's a small world" attraction

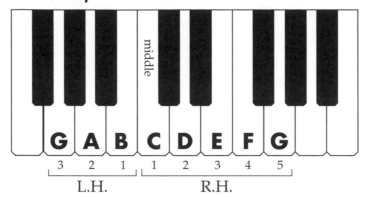

Play the *Small World Warm-Up* first to practice the skips in the melody.

Small World Warm-Up

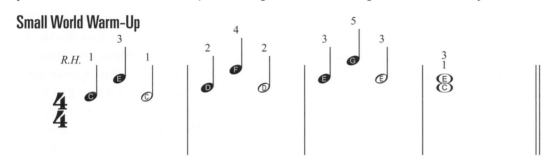

**Words and Music by Richard M. Sherman
and Robert B. Sherman**

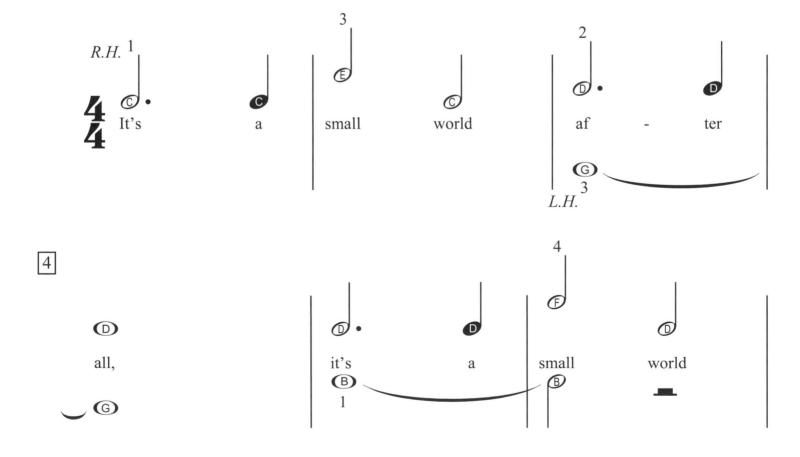

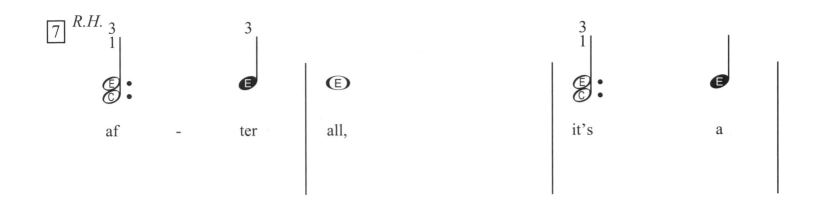

7 _R.H._

af - ter | all, | it's a

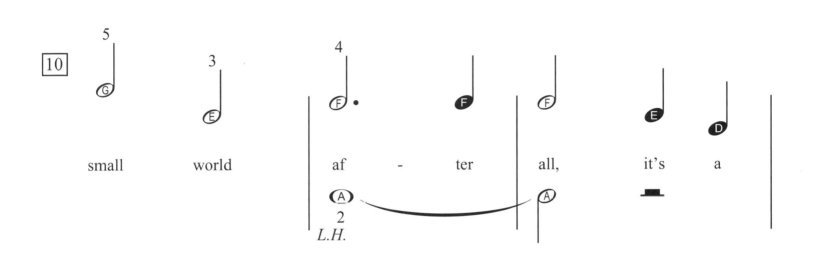

10

small world | af - ter | all, it's a

_L.H._

13

small, | small world.

YOU ARE MY SUNSHINE

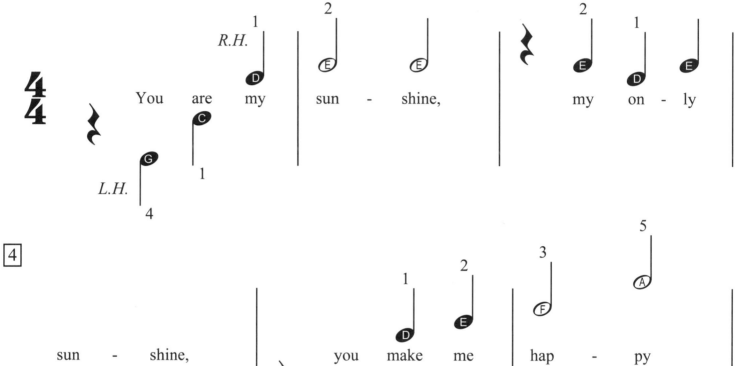

**Words and Music by
Jimmie Davis**

You are my | sun - shine, | my on - ly

sun - shine, | you make me | hap - py

Teacher Duet (Student plays one octave higher than written.)

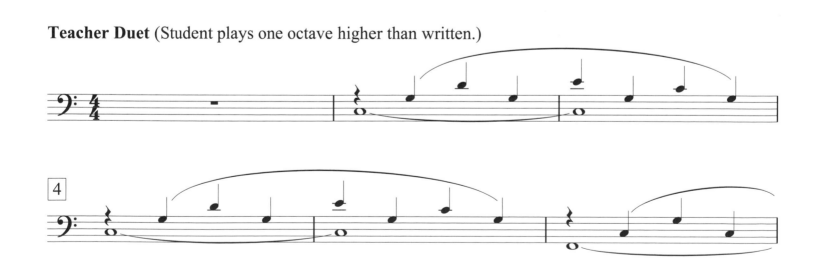

DO YOU WANT TO BUILD A SNOWMAN?

from FROZEN

Music and Lyrics by Kristen Anderson-Lopez
and Robert Lopez

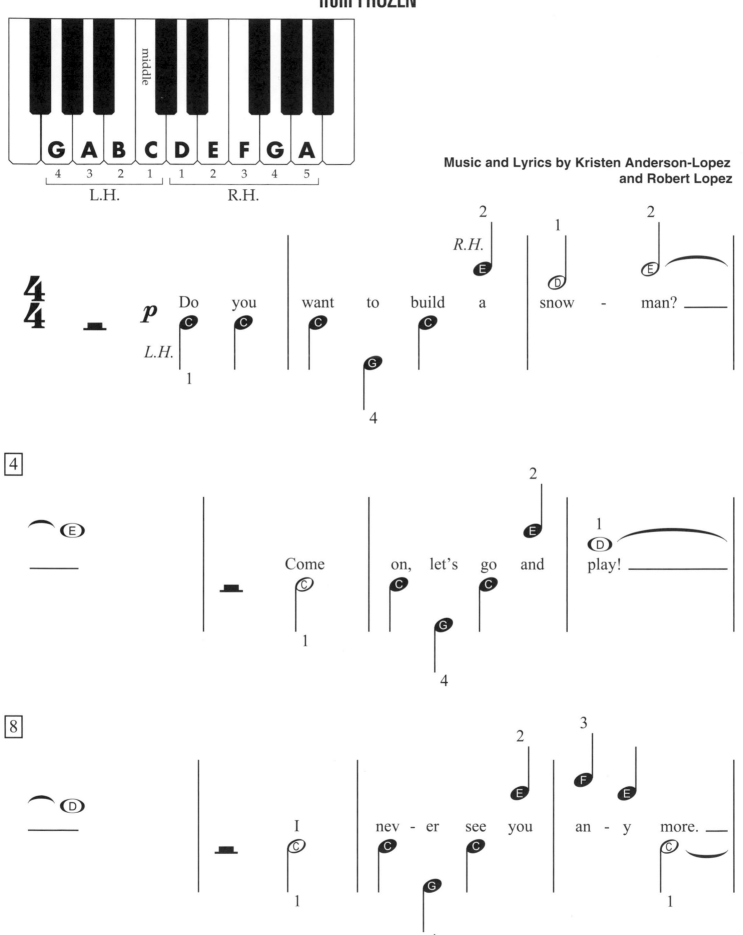

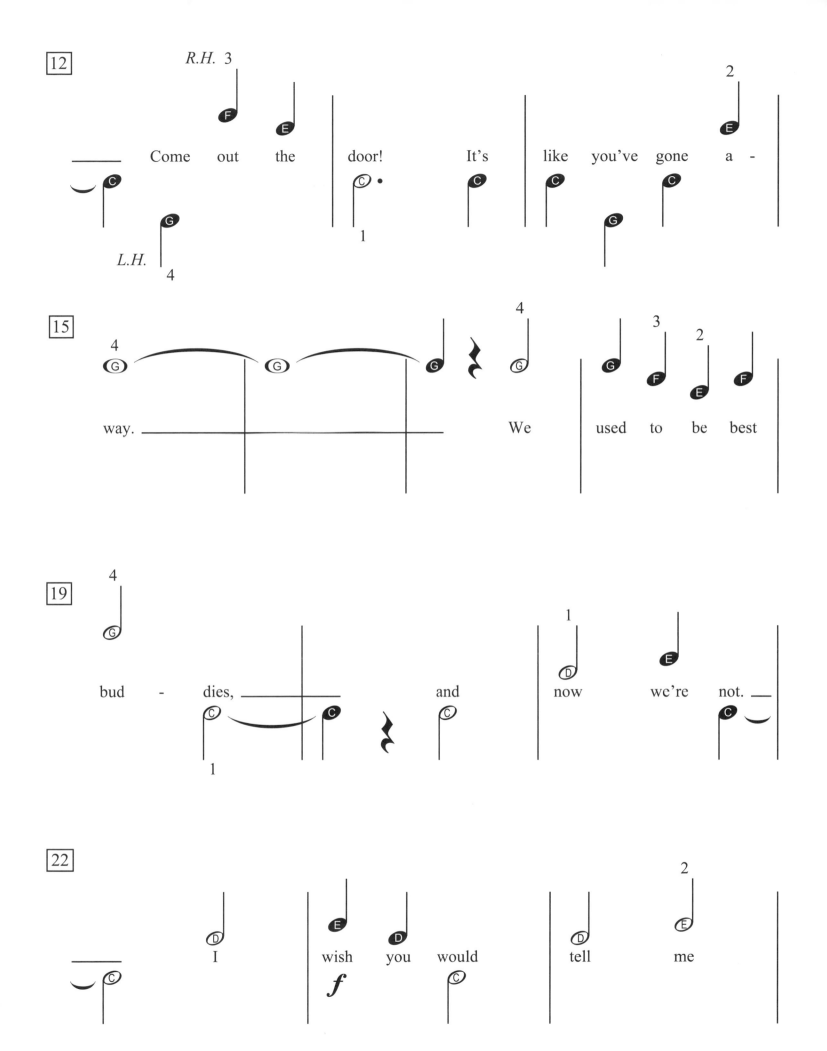

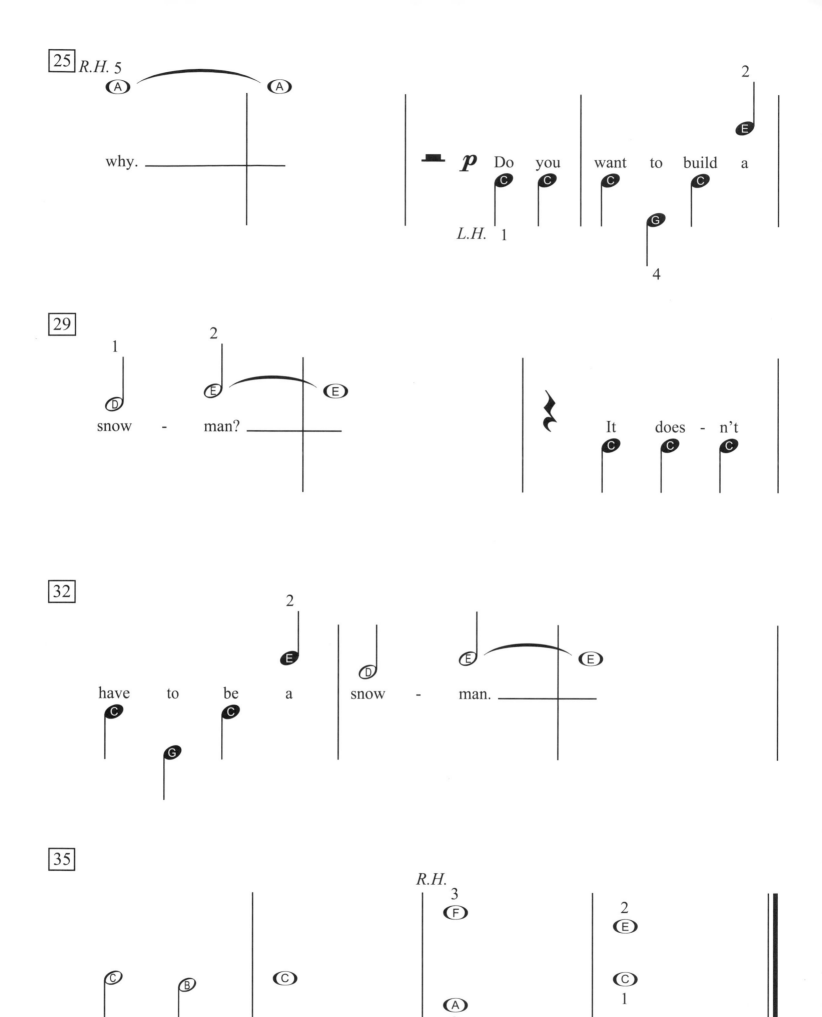

LINUS AND LUCY

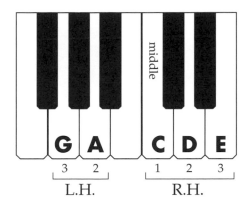

By Vince Guaraldi

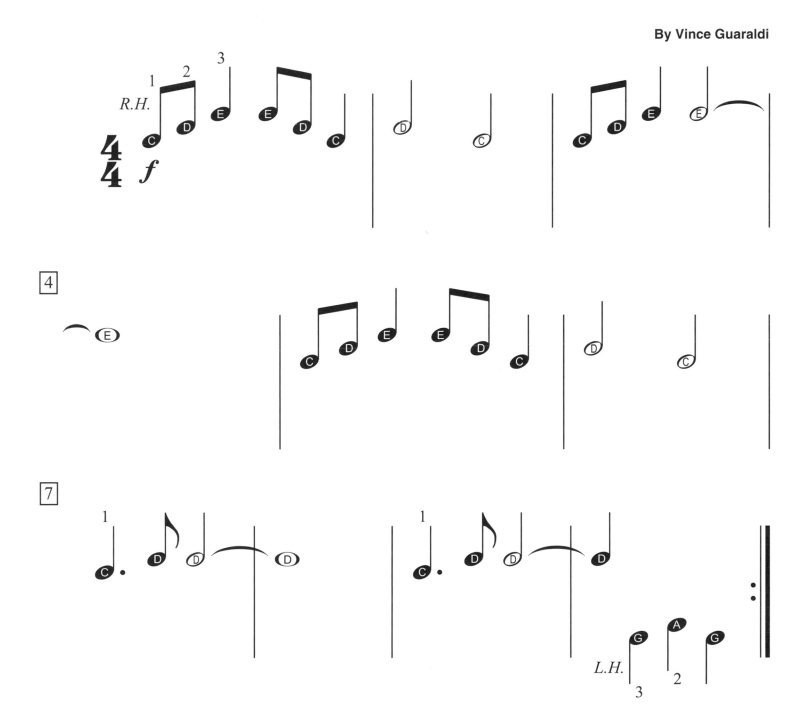

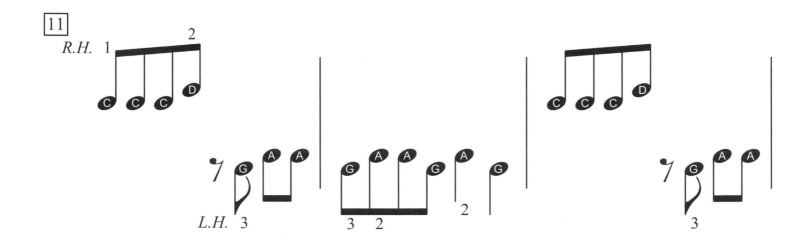

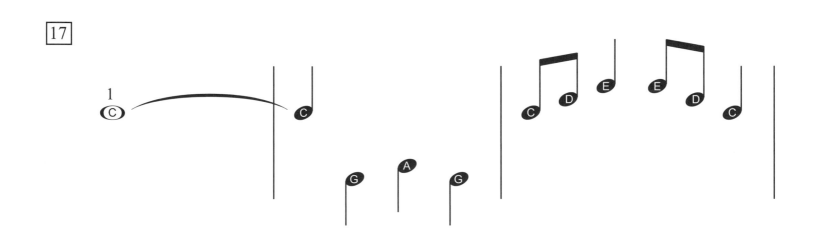

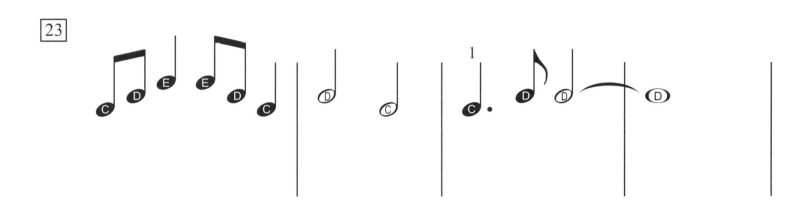

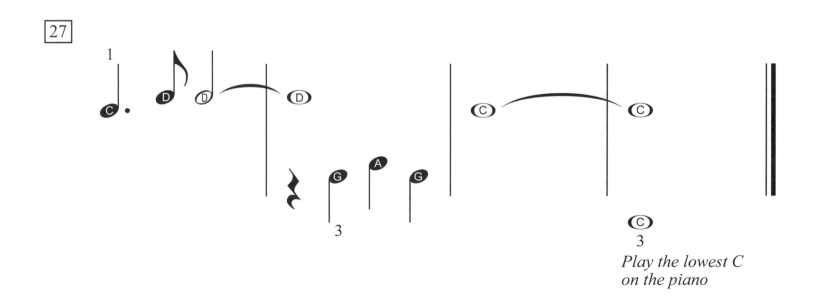

Play the lowest C on the piano

DOWN BY THE BAY

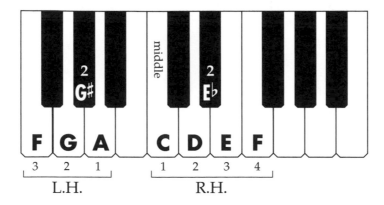

Words and Music by
Raffi Cavoukian

Down by the bay, where the wa-ter-mel-ons grow,

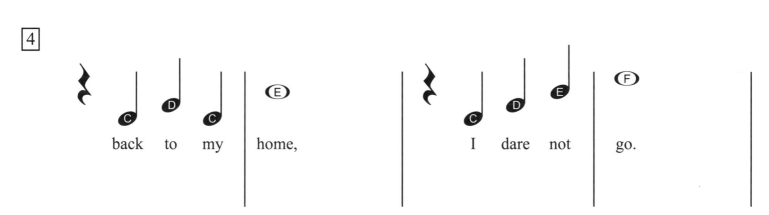

back to my home, I dare not go.

Teacher Duet (Student plays one octave higher than written.)

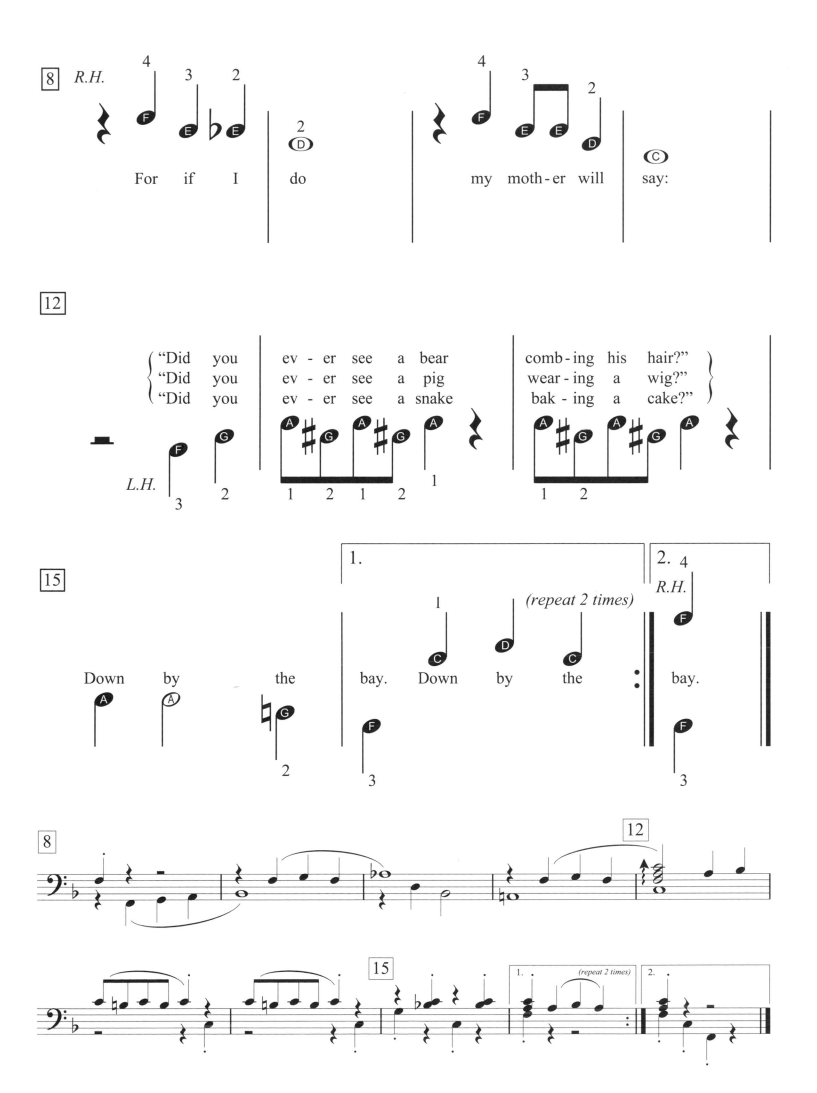

NOTESPELLNG ON THE GRAND STAFF

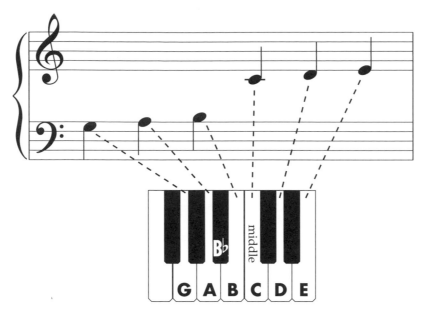

Write the correct note name in the blank below each note.

SUPERCALIFRAGILISTICEXPIALIDOCIOUS
from MARY POPPINS

**Words and Music by Richard M. Sherman
and Robert B. Sherman**

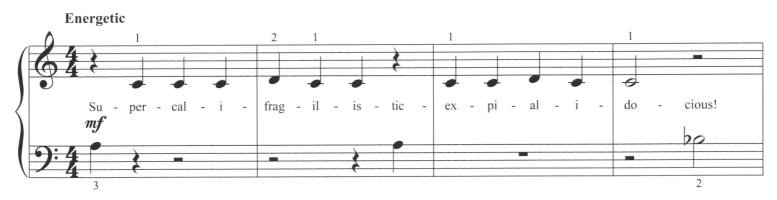

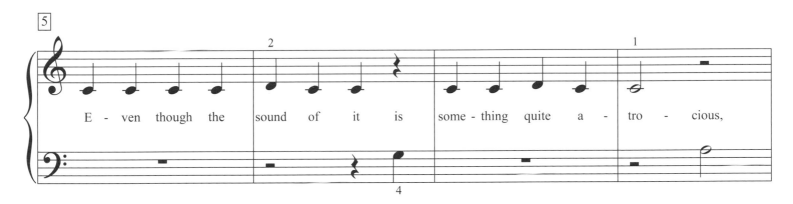

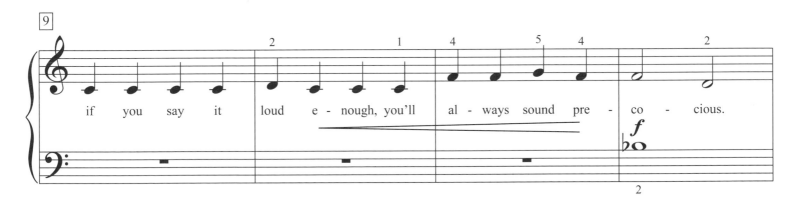

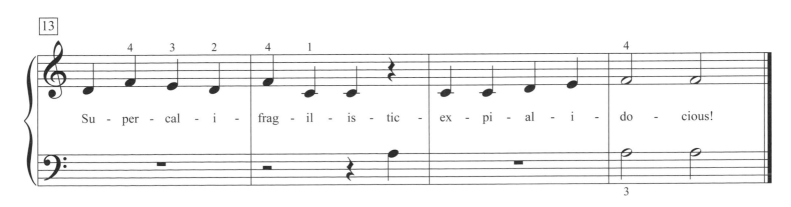

CAN'T STOP THE FEELING
from TROLLS

Words and Music by Justin Timberlake,
Max Martin and Shellback

Feel the groove in "2"

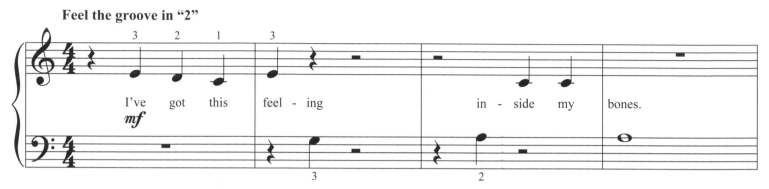

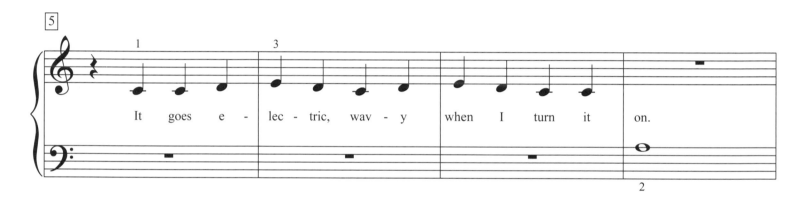

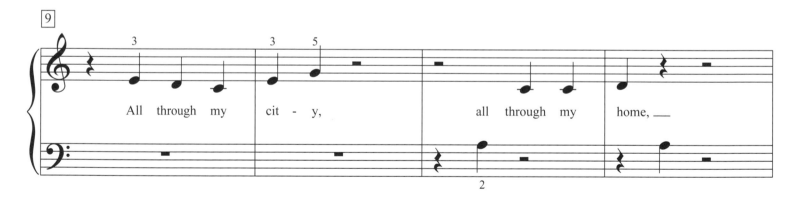

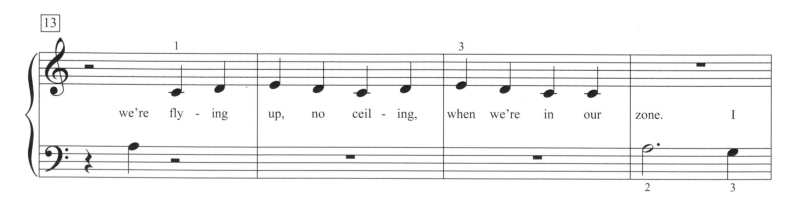

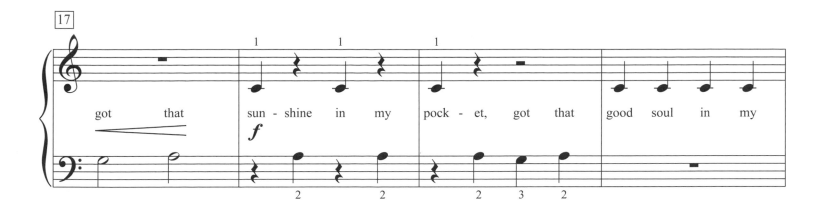

got that — sun- shine in my pock - et, got that good soul in my

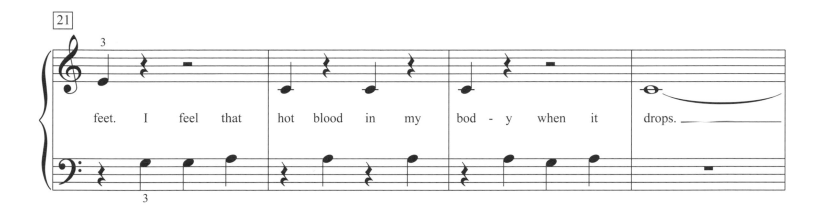

feet. I feel that hot blood in my bod - y when it drops. —

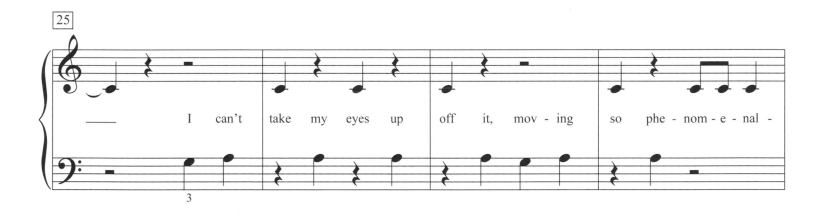

— I can't take my eyes up off it, mov - ing so phe - nom - e - nal -

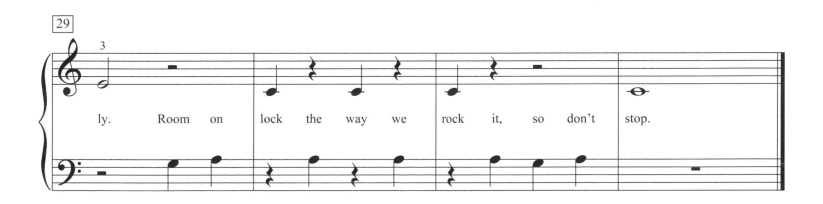

ly. Room on lock the way we rock it, so don't stop.

PIANO MAN

HAND POSITION SHIFT

In this book, when you see a ▲1 ▼1 fingering in a shaded triangle, your hand will need to move higher or lower on the keyboard depending on the direction of the triangle.

Words and Music by
Billy Joel

Moderately bright

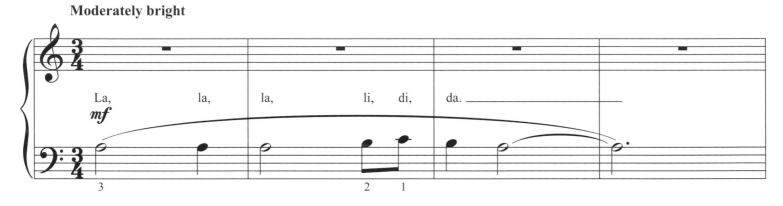

La, la, la, li, di, da.

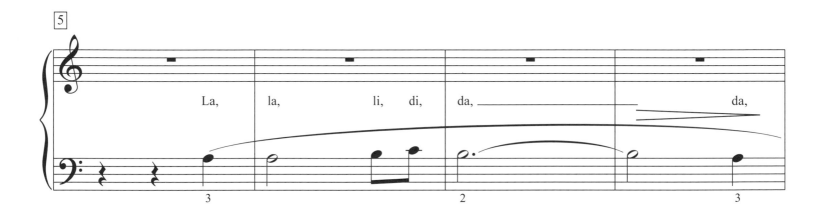

La, la, li, di, da, da,

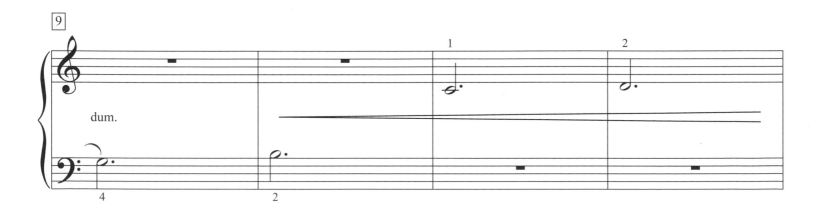

dum.

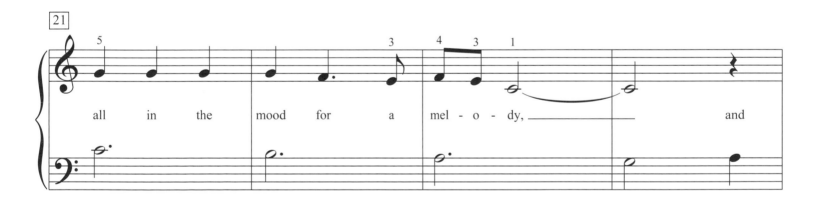

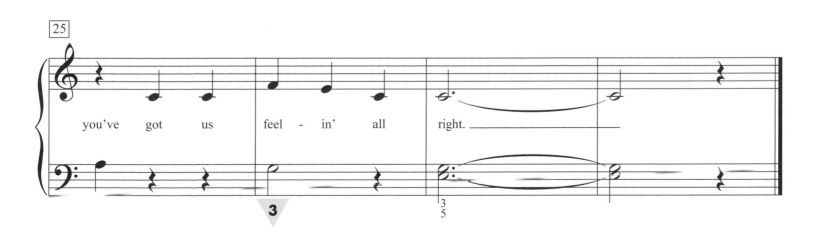

IF I DIDN'T HAVE YOU

from MONSTERS, INC.

Music and Lyrics by
Randy Newman

Moderate Swing

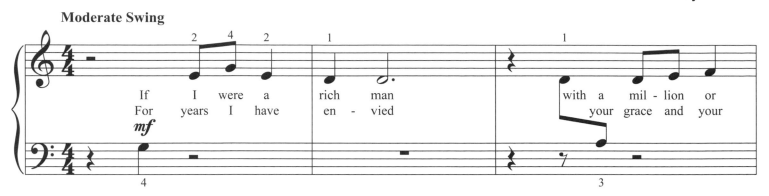

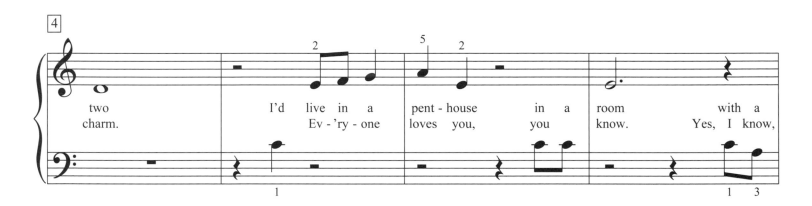

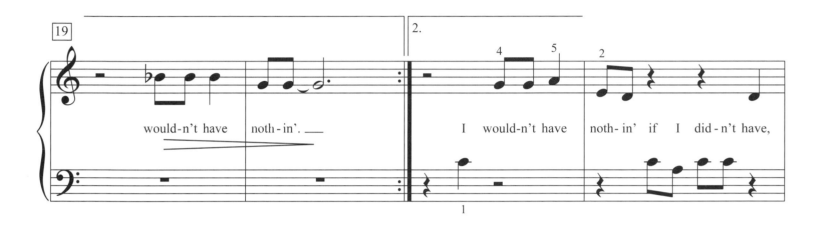

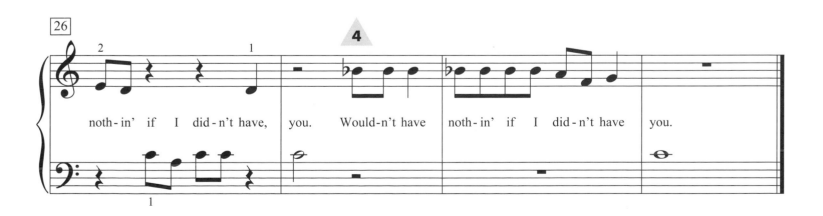

ALL OF ME

Words and Music by John Stephens
and Toby Gad

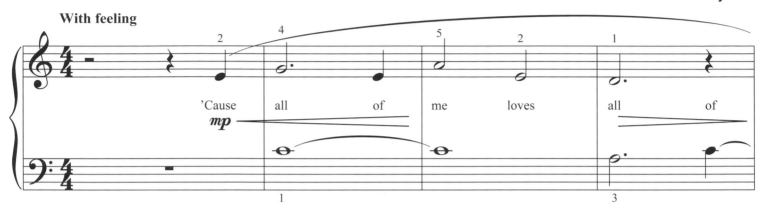

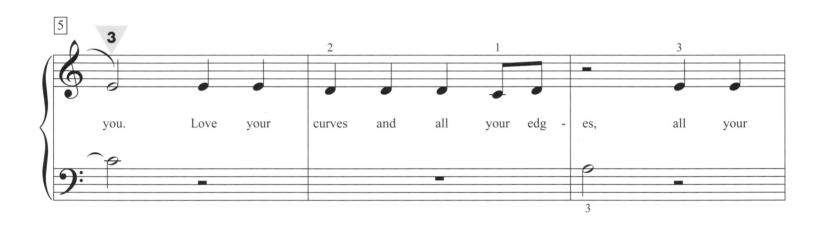

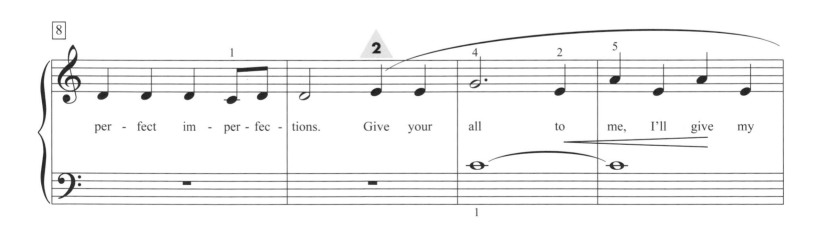

all   to   you.   You're my   end and my be - gin -

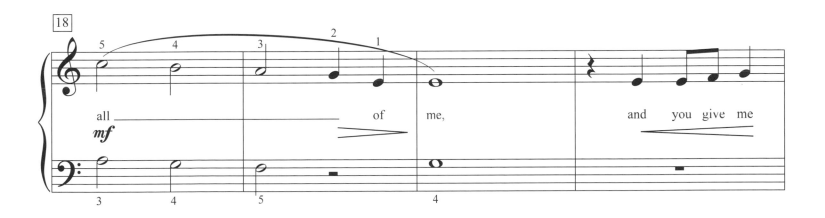

ning.   E - ven when I lose, I'm win - ning. 'Cause I give you

all   of   me,   and   you give me

mf

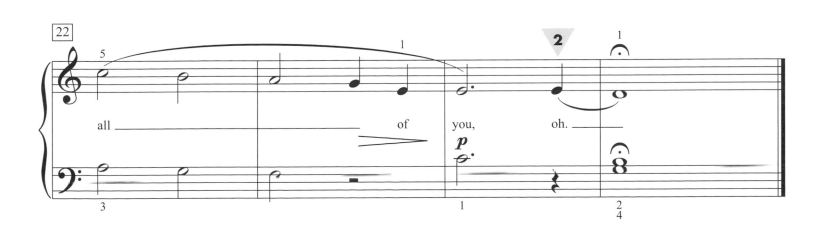

all   of   you,   oh.

p

DO-RE-MI
from THE SOUND OF MUSIC

Lyrics by Oscar Hammerstein II
Music by Richard Rodgers

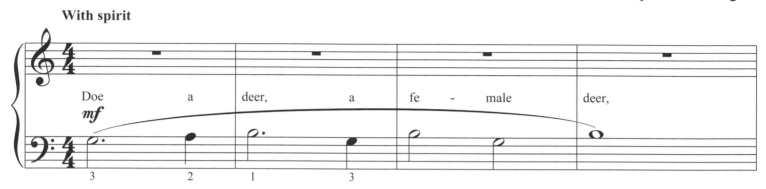

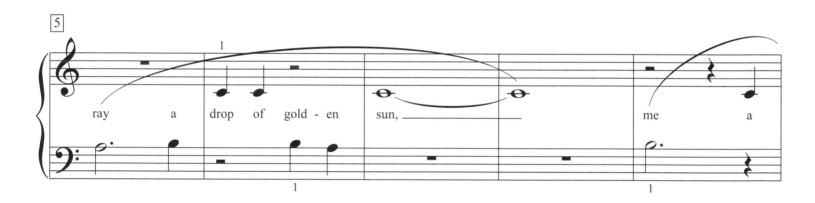

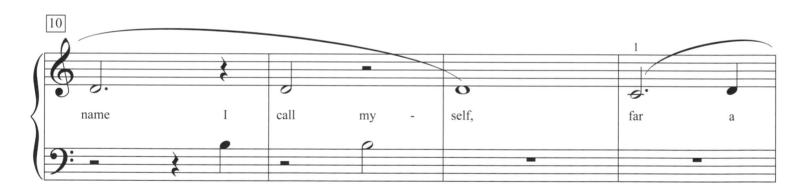

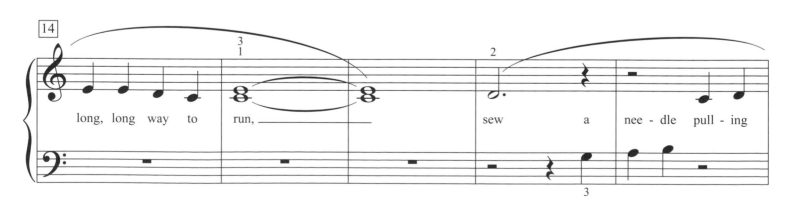

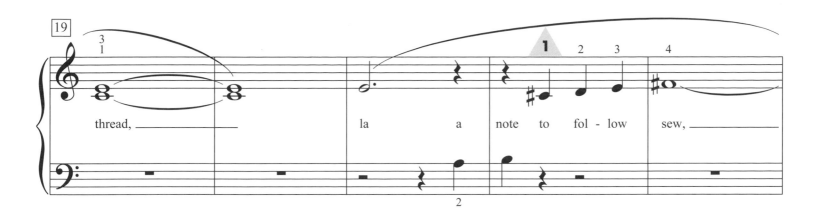

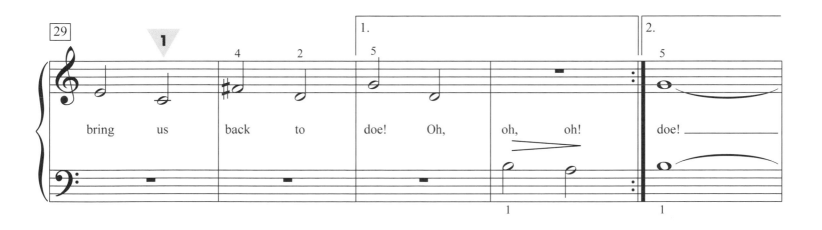

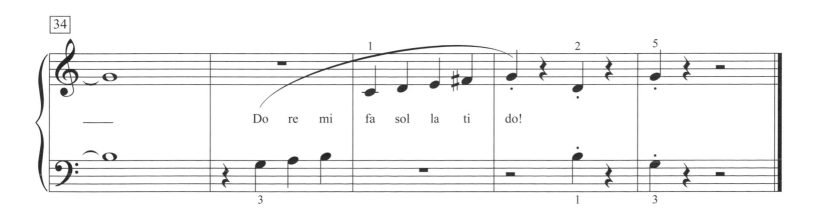

A WHOLE NEW WORLD
from ALADDIN

Music by Alan Menken
Lyrics by Tim Rice

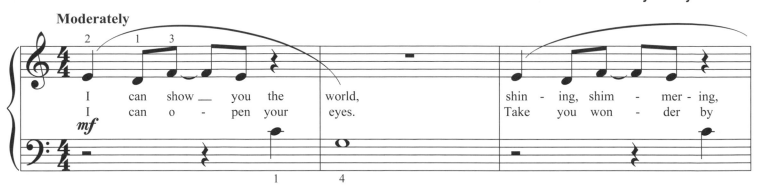

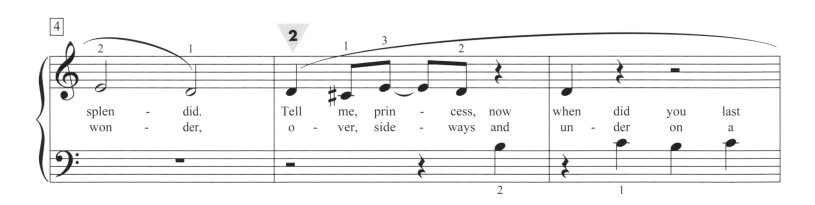

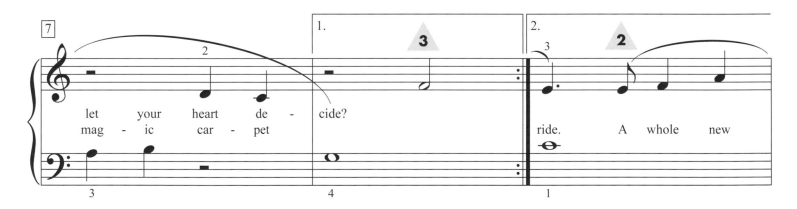

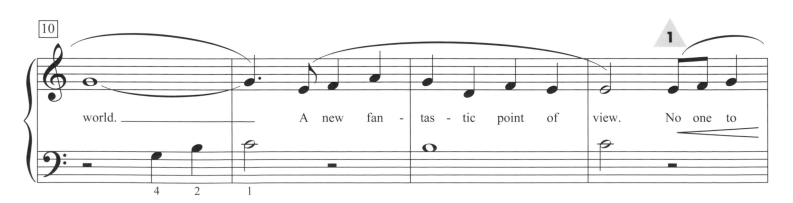

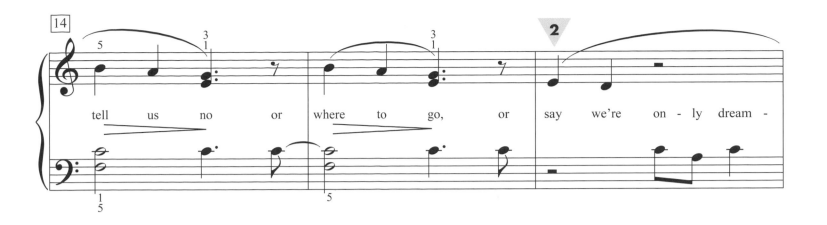

tell   us   no   or   where   to   go,   or   say   we're   on - ly   dream -

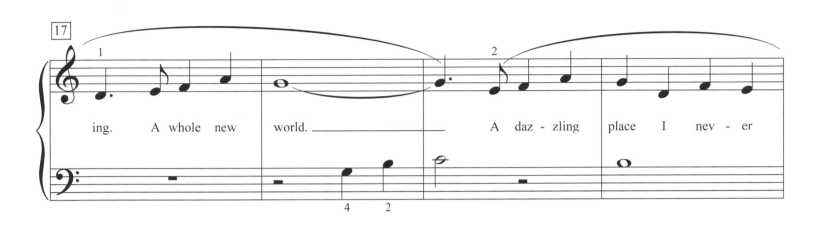

ing.   A   whole   new   world. _____   A   daz - zling   place   I   nev - er

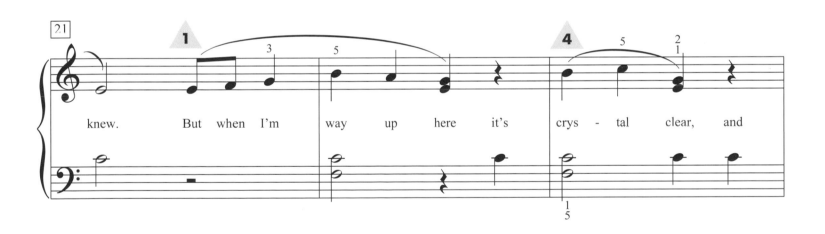

knew.   But   when   I'm   way   up   here   it's   crys - tal   clear,   and

now   I'm   in   a   whole   new   world   with   you.
rit.

PLAYING PIANO HAS NEVER BEEN EASIER!

5-Finger Piano Collections from Hal Leonard

BEATLES! BEATLES!

8 classics, including: A Hard Day's Night • Hey Jude • Love Me Do • P.S. I Love You • Ticket to Ride • Twist and Shout • Yellow Submarine • Yesterday.
00292061...$8.99

CHILDREN'S TV FAVORITES
Themes from 8 Hit Shows

Five-finger arrangements of the themes for: Barney • Bob the Builder • Thomas the Tank Engine • Dragon Tales • PB&J Otter • SpongeBob SquarePants • Rugrats • Dora the Explorer.
00311208...$7.95

CHURCH SONGS FOR KIDS

Features five-finger arrangements of 15 sacred favorites, including: Amazing Grace • The B-I-B-L-E • Down in My Heart • Fairest Lord Jesus • Hallelu, Hallelujah! • I'm in the Lord's Army • Jesus Loves Me • Kum Ba Yah • My God Is So Great, So Strong and So Mighty • Oh, How I Love Jesus • Praise Him, All Ye Little Children • Zacchaeus • and more.
00310613...$8.99

CLASSICAL FAVORITES – 2ND EDITION

Includes 12 beloved classical pieces from Bach, Bizet, Haydn, Grieg and other great composers: Bridal Chorus • Hallelujah! • He Shall Feed His Flock • Largo • Minuet in G • Morning • Rondeau • Surprise Symphony • To a Wild Rose • Toreador Song.
00310611...$8.99

DISNEY MOVIE FUN

8 classics, including: Beauty and the Beast • When You Wish Upon a Star • Whistle While You Work • and more.
00292067...$8.99

DISNEY TUNES

Includes: Can You Feel the Love Tonight? • Chim Chim Cher-ee • Go the Distance • It's a Small World • Supercalifragilisticexpialidocious • Under the Sea • You've Got a Friend in Me • Zero to Hero.
00310375...$8.99

SELECTIONS FROM DISNEY'S PRINCESS COLLECTION VOL. 1

7 songs sung by Disney heroines – with a full-color illustration of each! Includes: Colors of the Wind • A Dream Is a Wish Your Heart Makes • I Wonder • Just Around the Riverbend • Part of Your World • Something There • A Whole New World.
00310847 ....$8.99

EENSY WEENSY SPIDER & OTHER NURSERY RHYME FAVORITES

Includes 11 rhyming tunes kids love: Hickory Dickory Dock • Humpty Dumpty • Hush, Little Baby • Jack and Jill • Little Jack Horner • Mary Had a Little Lamb • Peter, Peter Pumpkin Eater • Pop Goes the Weasel • Tom, Tom, the Piper's Son • more.
00310465...$7.95

FIRST POP SONGS

Eight timeless pop classics are presented here in accessible arrangements: Candle in the Wind • Lean on Me • Moon River • Piano Man • Tears in Heaven • Unchained Melody • What a Wonderful World • Yellow Submarine.
00123296...$8.99

FROZEN
Music from the Motion Picture

Seven popular songs from *Frozen* are featured in single-note melody lines that stay in one position in this songbook. Songs include: Do You Want to Build a Snowman? • Fixer Upper • For the First Time in Forever • In Summer • Let It Go • Love Is an Open Door • Reindeer(s) Are Better Than People. Includes lyrics and beautifully-written accompaniments.
00130374...$10.99

MODERN MOVIE FAVORITES

Eight modern movie songs including lyrics: Can't Stop the Feeling • City of Stars • Evermore • Everything Is Awesome (Awesome Remixx!!!) • How Far I'll Go • Spirit in the Sky • Try Everything • Unforgettable.
00242674...$9.99

POP HITS FOR FIVE-FINGER PIANO

8 hot hits that even beginners can play, including: Cups (When I'm Gone) • Home • I Won't Give Up • Love Story • Next to Me • Skyfall • What Makes You Beautiful • When I Was Your Man. These books also include optional duet parts for a teacher or parent to play that makes the student sound like a pro!
00123295...$9.99

THE SOUND OF MUSIC

8 big-note arrangements of popular songs from this perennial favorite musical, including: Climb Ev'ry Mountain • Do-Re-Mi • Edelweiss • The Lonely Goatherd • My Favorite Things • Sixteen Going on Seventeen • So Long, Farewell • The Sound of Music.
00310249...$10.99

SELECTIONS FROM *STAR WARS*
arr. Robert Schultz

Based on the fantastic series of *Star Wars* movies, these songs were carefully selected and arranged by Robert Schultz at the five finger level. Included in the folio are: Anakin's Theme • Augie's Great Municipal Band • Cantina Band • Duel of the Fates • The Imperial March • Luke and Leia • Princess Leia's Theme • Star Wars (Main Title) • Yoda's Theme.
00321903...$9.99

www.halleonard.com